Eastbury Manor House, Barking

EASTBURY MANOR HOUSE
BY J. C. BUCKLER (1823)

EASTBURY MANOR HOUSE, BARKING, BEING THE ELEVENTH MONOGRAPH OF THE LONDON SURVEY COMMITTEE, WITH DRAWINGS BY HUBERT V. C. CURTIS.

MEMBERS OF THE LONDON SURVEY COMMITTEE DURING THE PERIOD OF THE WORK

THE FORMER PRESIDENTS OF THE COMMITTEE WERE—
THE LATE LORD LEIGHTON, P.R.A.
THE LATE RIGHT HON AND RIGHT REV. DR. CREIGHTON, LORD BISHOP OF LONDON

President

THE RIGHT HON THE EARL CURZON OF KEDLESTON, K G, G C S I, G.C.I.E, F R.S

Honorary Members.

THE RIGHT HON LORD ABERDARE
THE BOARD OF AGRICULTURE
SIR ROBERT ALLISON, M P
THE SOCIETY OF ANTIQUARIES
WILLIAM SUMNER APPLETON
THE ROYAL INSTITUTE OF BRITISH ARCHITECTS
THE SOCIETY OF ARCHITECTS
THE ARCHITECTURAL ASSOCIATION.
THE ATHENÆUM
JOHN AVERY, F C A, F.S S
E BURRELL BAGGALLAY
E. J. BARRON, F S A
BOYLSTON A BEAL
THE BERMONDSEY PUBLIC LIBRARIES
THE VEN ARCHDEACON HENRY E J BEVAN
HENRY FORBES BIGELOW.
ARTHUR L BILHAM
HARRY W. BIRKS
THE BIRMINGHAM CENTRAL LIBRARY
THE BISHOPSGATE INSTITUTE
E W BROOKS
A HERVÉ BROWNING
SIR WILLIAM BULL, M P
THE WORSHIPFUL COMPANY OF CARPENTERS
MISS A G. E CARTHEW.
W J. CHECKLEY.
THE CHELSEA PUBLIC LIBRARY.
THE CHISWICK PUBLIC LIBRARY
CYRIL S COBB, M V.O
E C COLQUHOUN.
THE COLUMBIA UNIVERSITY LIBRARY
THE CONSTITUTIONAL CLUB
WILLIAM W CORDINGLEY
THE RIGHT HON. LORD COURTNEY OF PENWITH, P C
THE RIGHT HON THE EARL OF CRAWFORD, F S A
W E VERNON CROMPTON.
THE CROYDON PUBLIC LIBRARY
S HORACE DENMAN
GEORGE H DUCKWORTH, F S A
THE BOARD OF EDUCATION.
EUSTACE ERLEBACH
THE RIGHT HON. THE EARL FERRERS
LENNARD W. FORSYTH
SIR GEORGE FRAMPTON, R A, F S A
MISS AGNES GARRETT
W S GODFREY
SIR RICKMAN J GODLEE, K C V O
GOLDSMITHS' LIBRARY, UNIVERSITY OF LONDON.

Honorary Members—continued

A GRAY, K C
Miss I. I. GREAVES
HUBERT J GREENWOOD, L C C.
Major-Gen. Sir COLERIDGE GROVE, K C B
The GUILDHALL LIBRARY
The HACKNEY PUBLIC LIBRARY.
RICHARD WALDEN HALE
EDWIN T HALL, F R I B A
The HAMMERSMITH CENTRAL LIBRARY.
Mrs HENRY HANKEY
ROWLAND G HAZARD
Sir SAMUEL HOARE, Bt, M P
V. T HODGSON
J J HOLDSWORTH
CHARLES H HOPWOOD, F S A
E J HORNIMAN
Miss LOIS L HOWE.
DOUGLAS ILLINGWORTH
Mrs ILLINGWORTH ILLINGWORTH
The Right Hon. the VISCOUNT IVEAGH, K P, G C V.O, F R S
EDWARD TYRRELL JAQUES
GILBERT JENKINS.
C H. F KINDERMANN.
C L KINGSFORD
G C LAWSON
The Right Hon the Lady LECONFIELD
The Right Hon LORD LEVERHULME, M.P.
OWEN C. LITTLE
The LONDON LIBRARY
Dr G B LONGSTAFF.
The Right Hon MARY, COUNTESS OF LOVELACE.
The MANCHESTER PUBLIC LIBRARY

WILLIAM McGREGOR.
Mrs JOHN MARKOE
Miss B A MEINERTZHAGEN.
The METROPOLITAN PUBLIC GARDENS ASSOCIATION
G VAUGHAN MORGAN
Mrs JOHN H MORRISON
JOHN MURRAY, F R I.B A.
JAMES A NELSON
The NEW YORK PUBLIC LIBRARY
Mrs RICHARD NICHOLSON.
R C NORMAN
Mrs ROBERT NORMAN
The Rev J P NOYES
VERE L OLIVER
The OXFORD AND CAMBRIDGE CLUB.
F. W PETERS
The FREE LIBRARY, PHILADELPHIA
Mrs W WILTON PHIPPS
F W PLATT
D'ARCY POWER, F R C S.
Sir E J POYNTER, Bt, K C V.O, P R.A, F.S A
F W PROCTER
The PUBLIC RECORD OFFICE
COLIN E READER.
The REFORM CLUB
Mrs F L W RICHARDSON.
The SHOREDITCH PUBLIC LIBRARY
SION COLLEGE
Mrs VERNON SMITH
A G SNELGROVE
W J SONGHURST.
H C SOTHERAN
The SOUTHWARK PUBLIC LIBRARY.
The STOKE NEWINGTON PUBLIC LIBRARY
R CLIPSTON STURGIS

4

Honorary Members—continued

The Right Hon LORD ALEXANDER BOTEVILLE THYNNE, M P
A. GRAYSTONE WARREN
The LIBRARY OF CONGRESS, WASHINGTON.
The WEST HAM PUBLIC LIBRARY.
Mrs WESTLAKE
The WESTMINSTER PUBLIC LIBRARY
Mrs. WHARRIE.
J. BARRINGTON WHITE
Miss M J WILDE
JOHN E YERBURY
KEITH D YOUNG, F R I B A

Active Members

C. R ASHBEE, M.A.
OSWALD BARRON, F.S A.
A. H BLAKE, M A
*W W BRAINES, B A (Lond)
A. E BULLOCK, A R I B A
G H CHETTLE
*A W CLAPHAM, F S A
*GEORGE CLINCH, F G S, F S.A (Scot)
A O COLLARD, A R I B A
F. T DEAR
WILLIAM DODDINGTON
H W. FINCHAM
MATT GARBUTT
Mrs. ERNEST GODMAN, A R I
T FRANK GREEN, A R I B A.
EDWIN GUNN, A.R I.B A.
OSBORN C HILLS, F R I B A
E. W HUDSON
T. GORDON-JACKSON, Licentiate R I B.A
MAX JUDGE
P K KIPPS, A R I B A
GILBERT H LOVEGROVE
ERNEST A. MANN, Licentiate R.I B A
E T MARRIOTT, M A.
CECIL G McDOWELL
W MONK, R E
SYDNEY NEWCOMBE
E C NISBET.
*ROBERT PEARSALL
*FRANCIS W READER.
ERNEST RAILTON
JOHN RAVENSHAW
JOSEPH SEDDON.
*FRANCIS R. TAYLOR, Licentiate R I B A.
GEORGE TROTMAN
Miss E. M B WARREN
W A. WEBB, A R I B A
*W. WONNACOTT, A R I B A
E L WRATTEN, A R I B A
*EDWARD YATES.
*W. P YOUNG
*PHILIP NORMAN, F S A, LL D, *Editor of the Committee*
E L MEINERTZHAGEN, J P, L C C, *Treasurer of the Committee*
PERCY LOVELL, B A, A R I B A, *Secretary of the Committee*
*WALTER H. GODFREY, F S A, *Acting Secretary of the Committee*, 27, Abingdon Street, Westminster, S W 1

* *Members who have assisted in the present work*

CONTENTS.

	PAGE
MEMBERS OF THE SURVEY COMMITTEE	3
DESCRIPTION OF THE PLATES	7
PREFACE	9
HISTORICAL NOTES	13
ARCHITECTURAL DESCRIPTION	19
BIBLIOGRAPHICAL NOTES	30
INDEX	33

DESCRIPTION OF THE PLATES.

Plate 1 (Frontispiece)—Sketch in 1823 - - J C Buckler
       2 Sketch from south - - By Hubert V C Curtis

MEASURED DRAWINGS.

Plate 3 Ground and first floor plans - By Hubert V C Curtis
       4 Roof and second floor plans, and section - - - - By Hubert V. C Curtis
       5 Cross section - - - By Hubert V C Curtis
       6 North elevation - - - By Hubert V C Curtis
       7 South elevation - - - By Hubert V C Curtis
       8 East elevation - - - By Hubert V C Curtis
       9. Detail of porch and north gable By Hubert V C Curtis
    10 Porch and door - - - - By T. H Clarke
    11 Detail of chimney stack - - By Hubert V. C. Curtis
    12 Details of mouldings, etc - By Hubert V C Curtis
    13 Chimney-piece, east wing, first floor - By F R Taylor
    14. Panelled room, ground floor - By Hubert V C. Curtis

PHOTOGRAPHS.

Plate 15. South front - - - - - By Edward Yates
    16. ,, ,. from S.W. - - - By F R. Taylor
    17 ,, ,, from S E - - - By F R. Taylor
    18 West front and S.W. gable - - By W Wonnacott
    19 East and north fronts - - - By Edward Yates
    20 Porch - - - - - By F. R Taylor
    21. { (a) Arch under chimney-stack - - By Edward Yates
          { (b) Corbelling to chimney-stack - By W P. Young
    22. Stair turret and chimney-stack - By Edward Yates
    23. Stair turret, door - - - - By W. Wonnacott
    24. Roofs and chimney-stack - - By Edward Yates
    25. { (a) Windows in gable - - By W. P. Young
          { (b) Garden entrance - - - By Edward Yates
    26 Panelled room, ground floor - - By F. R Taylor
    27. { (a) Fireplace, first floor - - By W. P. Young
          { (b) ,, detail - - - By W P Young

PHOTOGRAPHS—*continued*.

Plate 28.
- (*a*) Second floor, roof - - - By Edward Yates
- (*b*) ,, ,, - - - By Edward Yates
- (*c*) ,, ,, staircase - - By Edward Yates

29. Barn, interior - - - - By F. R. Taylor

PAINTINGS.

Plate 30. Painted room, west side - Drawn by T. H. Clarke
31. ,, ,, east side - Photograph
Lent by *Royal Commission on Historical Monuments (England)*
32. Painted gallery, second floor - Drawn by T. H. Clarke

ILLUSTRATIONS IN THE TEXT. Page

Back-plate of wrought-iron knocker Drawn by T. H. Clarke 12
Hinge and handle - - - ,, T. H. Clarke 18
Plan with garden - - - - ,, P. J. Marvin 20
Details from drawings in the Bodleian Library
Lent by *Messrs. B. T. Batsford, Ltd.* 21
Chimney-piece (hall) - - - Drawn by T. H. Clarke 23
,, ,, (N.E. room, ground floor)
Drawn by T. H. Clarke 25
,, ,, (Painted room over hall)
Drawn by T. H. Clarke 26
,, ,, (West room over hall) ,, T. H. Clarke 27
Figures from the painted gallery - - Ogborne's "History of Essex" - 28
Seal of Barking Abbey - - - - - - - 36

HERALDIC ILLUSTRATIONS.

Denham.—*Gules*, three lozenges, *Ermine* - - - - 14
Sisley.—*Azure*, on a cheveron between three goats *Argent*, armed *Or*, three fleurs-de-lys *Azure* - - - - 16
More (Chester).—*Ermine*, between six cocks a fess *Gules* - 26

PREFACE.

THE record of Eastbury Manor House as presented in these pages is not merely the eleventh of the Committee's Historical Monographs,—those responsible for it have a particular object in view, it is intended to reinforce the very strong appeal that is being made for funds to purchase and preserve this beautiful building When the propriety of continuing its publications during the present world-conflict was discussed by the Committee, what weighed most in the balance was the grave danger which even now is threatening many of our own national and historical memorials Even when we are condemning an enemy's ruthless vandalism in France and Belgium the ancient buildings of our Capital and of Greater London enjoy no immunity from danger, and to be consistent we must not cease to combat the forces of destruction at home, although they may proceed from mere thoughtlessness and ignorance rather than from a considered policy of evil

The last year or so has seen the quiet row of early eighteenth-century houses in Old Queen Street, Westminster, swept away, while Queen Anne's Gate itself has been threatened Bolingbroke House, Battersea, is to be given over to the housebreakers Even our sacred buildings are not safe, a direct attack on the mediæval church of St Olave, Hart Street—linked so closely with the name of Pepys—was happily averted only just in time These considerations and the news of the sale of Eastbury Manor House—long neglected, but so greatly prized by all who know its value—determined the Committee to press on with its work, and the choice of the subject for the present volume was immediately made.

We are glad to be able to state that the new owner of Eastbury is quite in sympathy with the scheme which has been formulated for the repair of the building and its preservation in trust for the nation He has offered very generous terms for its purchase, and the Society for the Protection of Ancient Buildings has undertaken the task of raising the money in order that the house and grounds may be conveyed to the National Trust for Places of Historic Interest or Natural Beauty Some £3,000 will be required to purchase and fit the building for some worthy public object, and now that the opportunity has occurred which all lovers of architecture have desired ever since W H Black wrote his account of the house in 1834, it is of the utmost importance that the scheme should be carried through without delay With judicious repair Eastbury can be saved, and we hope that everyone who is able, and whom these pages remind of the value of the object in view, will aid according to his means. In these days of change every bit of Old England is worthy of preservation, and it is not often that an opportunity occurs of preserving for all time so complete and striking an example of a Tudor manor house.

Pictorial records of Eastbury are fairly numerous, and a list of them is given in the Bibliography here printed. Thomas Hutchings Clarke contributed a fine series of measured drawings and views to a book produced jointly with W. H Black in 1834. A competition, held under the auspices of the Royal Institute of British Architects, for measured drawings illustrating the restoration of Eastbury occurred in 1871-72, at the instance of Mr H W Peek, M.P (Hon. Fellow R I B A), who offered prizes of £42 and £20. Mr. T E C. Streatfeild won the first prize, and his historical essay was published in the R I B.A. Transactions for 8 April, 1872. Mr P J Marvin was the second prize winner, and his drawings have since appeared in the Architectural Association Sketch Book, 1903, 3rd Series, vol. vii. Medals of merit were awarded to Mr H. Avern and to the late Mr Walter L Spiers, who was an enthusiastic member of our Committee, and whose recent death we have had to deplore. One of Mr Avern's drawings appeared in the Architectural Association Sketch Book, 1871-72, vol. vi, and Mr. Spiers' original drawings are preserved in his brother's collection at the Victoria and Albert Museum, South Kensington. One of our present active members was also a competitor, Mr. Robert Pearsall, who claims to have been first on the scene at Eastbury, and who has preserved some interesting notes of the buildings

The Committee has been fortunate in obtaining for the purposes of the present volume a new and complete set of drawings by Mr Hubert V C Curtis, who has kindly placed them at our disposal for reproduction. Such features as have vanished from the house are here shown from the drawings of T H Clarke, and are reproduced from the copy of this rare book, which has been lent to the Committee by Mr C J Dawson, of Barking. For one or two further illustrations we are indebted to Messrs. B T Batsford who have permitted their reproduction from Messrs Garner and Stratton's "Tudor Architecture." Mr Marvin has lent his plan of the house and garden. The sincere thanks of the Committee are due to these gentlemen, and also to the Chairman and Members of the Royal Commission on Historical Monuments (England) for permission to use a photograph of the paintings which are still visible on the walls of the room over the old hall. The bibliography has been prepared by Mr George Clinch

It will be easily understood that the production of this volume under present conditions has not been free from difficulty. We had to find time and money when our chief energies were absorbed in the great national effort which the European war calls forth. It will therefore not be considered out of place if I express my satisfaction at the unhesitating support which has been received from members of the Committee The special fund for the production of the volume received an immediate and gratifying response from a large number of our supporters, and the active workers have tried hard to produce a worthy record That these efforts shall bear fruit in the permanent preservation of the building is their earnest wish

PHILIP NORMAN.

BACK-PLATE OF WROUGHT-IRON KNOCKER.

SOME HISTORICAL NOTES.

EASTBURY HOUSE is in the parish of Barking and hundred of Becontree,* Essex. It is on the road to Dagenham through Rippleside, and the ground between it and the town of Barking has been much built over in recent years.

Before the Dissolution a considerable part of Becontree hundred belonged to the famous Benedictine Convent of Barking, which appears to have been founded before the year 675, and of which the ground plan has lately been recovered by Mr A. W. Clapham. We are not quite sure if, after the establishment of the feudal system, there was a Manor of Eastbury or not, but as there was a Manor of Westbury about a mile off, close to the town of Barking, it is most probable that the popular name for the house has some foundation in fact. Moreover, according to W. H. Black,† in an old survey of Essex, *temp* James I., it is called the Manor of Eastbury Hall. Both Eastbury and Westbury would thus have been subsidiary manors, subject to the lordship of Barking. According to Black: "The Abbey was dissolved and its possessions surrendered to the King 14 November, 1539, after which £21 13s. 4d. was paid as a yearly rent to the Crown for six years, and the following entry thereof is contained in an account of one of the receivers of the Court of Augmentations:—'Estburie Firma Mesuagii, etc., £21 13s. 4d.'" This, he thinks, was the old rent paid to the Abbey under a lease that continued until the Crown sold off the estate, and the entry confirms the belief that a house existed on or near the site of the present one before the Dissolution. At Michaelmas, 1545, the Eastbury estate, together with the Manor of Westbury, was bought by Sir William Denham, who in the previous year had obtained a grant of thirteen houses in the parishes of St Olave Jewry and St Mary Staining, London, which had also been part of the Abbey's possessions. Sir William, son of Nicholas and Elizabeth Denham, of good family,‡ was born at Lyston, Devonshire, and going to London to make his way in commerce became a prominent citizen. He was sheriff in 1534–35 and was knighted 2nd February, 1542, being one of the very few aldermen in the sixteenth century who was thus honoured without passing the chair.§ That autumn, after

---

* *Spelt Beacon-tree by W. H. Black in "Eastbury, Illustrated, etc.," by T. H. Clarke and W. H. Black, 1834.*
† *Ibid., page 16, where he quotes from Harl. MS., 5, 195.*
‡ *See his pedigree in Nicholl's "History of the Ironmongers' Company," derived from visitations of Devon and Harleian MSS. The name seems to have been often spelt Dinham.*
§ *Beaven's "Aldermen of the City of London," 2 vols., 1908–13.*

Denham

being for eleven years alderman of Coleman Street Ward, he obtained his discharge at the King's request, but had to pay a fine. He was a great benefactor of the Ironmongers' Company, being master no less than seven times, and also made a bequest to the Grocers'. He was evidently connected with the parish of All Hallows, Barking, and there still remains on a plain stone, without arms or effigy, in the north aisle of that church, the following inscription* in Gothic lettering, to his wife and himself:—

> "In this vawte here under lithe Elizabeth, late wife unto William Denham, Aldreman of London, and Marchaunt of the Staple of Caleys, who departed unto God on Wednesday at 5 of ye clok at afternoun Ester Weke ye last day of Marche Ao Di 1540
>
> "And by ye grace of God ye said William De'ham purporteth to lie by her, who departed unto God ye day of
> Ao Di."

The date of his death has never been filled in.

Morant† says that Denham held Eastbury at the time of his decease "with the appurtenances, viz., 200 acres of arable, 300 acres of pasture, 50 of meadow, 60 of wood, 200 of furze and heath".‡

The Rev. E. L. Cutts§ also speaks of his dying three years after he acquired the property, and T. E. C. Streatfeild‖ follows suit.

In his "History of the Ironmongers' Company,"¶ Mr John Nicholl, F.S.A., gives some useful information about Sir William Denham, including brief epitomes of his two wills. Of the first, dated 12th September, 1544 (36 Henry VIII.), but for some unexplained reason not proved until 11th June, 1557, there is also an abstract in Dr. Reginald Sharpe's "Calendar of Wills," proved in the Court of Husting, from which we will now quote. As he explains in a note, it appears to have

---

* *The stone is still to be seen in the floor of the north aisle near the east end With trifling variations the Rev. J. Maskell, 1864, and a writer in the "Gentleman's Magazine," Vol. XCVI, agree in the wording given above*

† *Hist. Antiq. Essex, 768. He gives as his authority, Inq. 2 Edward VI (1548).*

‡ *Mr John Nicholl ("History of the Ironmongers' Company") says, at the time of Denham's decease, he held "13 messuages in London" and "the Manor of Eastbury and Westbury, containing 1,200 acres of arable land 900 of pasture, 150 of meadow, 140 of wood, and 700 of heath and furze with a portion of the tithes, all part and parcel of the possessions of the dissolved monastery of Barking"*

§ *"Proceedings Essex Arch Soc.," Vol. II, 1863, p 134*

‖ *Paper in R I B A Transactions, 1871-2*

¶ *Second edition, 1867*

14

been intended to take effect immediately after its execution and not from the time of Sir William's death. He leaves his London messuages in the parishes of St Olave Jewry and St Mary Staining to the Ironmongers' Company, charged with an annual payment to him or his assigns of £20 during his lifetime, and after his decease, with the observance of his obit within the chapel or within the parish church of "Our Ladie Barkinge" in Tower Ward, for the good of his soul, the souls of Nicholas and Elizabeth, his father and mother, and others, as in manner directed. Also they are to pay yearly the sum of forty-one shillings to the parson and churchwardens of Lyston, co Devon, where he was born, for pious uses, ten shillings to the "Wardens and Commonaltie of Grocerie" to the intent that their clerk or beadle attend his mass. In default made in carrying out the terms of his mass, the whole of the above property to go to the "Wardens and Commonaltie of Grocerie" aforesaid for similar uses, and in case of further default to his right heirs. Attention should be drawn to the fact already mentioned that the Barking property was not purchased until the following year.

On the 3rd of August, 1548, a day only before his death, Sir William Denham, having perhaps joined the reformed faith, made another will (deposited in the Prerogative Court of Canterbury) wherein he requests to be buried in the church of Barking* and appoints as executors his son-in-law William Abbott and his daughter Margery, wife of the said William, and devises to him and her and her heirs all the lands and houses which he minded that the Ironmongers should have, and all other lands and tenements whatsoever. He bequeaths legacies to the family of Breame and commits Grace his natural daughter to the safe keeping of William and Margery Abbott. In consequence of his second will the Ironmongers were obliged to purchase the London property before devised to them, as appears by a deed dated 27th May, 1567, the then owner being Arthur Breame, described as cousin of Sir William Denham

According to W H Black,† Sir William Denham's daughter, Margery Abbott, died within eight months of his decease. Her husband, William Abbott,‡ appears to have sold Eastbury to John Keele in 1557, and on the 7th May§ of the same year John Keele had leave to alienate the messuage, tenement or farm called Esbury in Barking to Clement Sisley, whose arms, granted 31st December, 1560, were *Azure*, on a cheveron between three goats passant *Argent*, armed *Or*, as many

---

* i e , *All Hallows, near the Tower*
† "*Eastbury, Illustrated, etc ,*" 1834
‡ *R I B A Transactions*, 1872, *Paper by* T E C *Streatfeild.*
§ *Morant, quoting Letters Patent* 3 & 4 *Philip and Mary.*

fleurs-de-lys of the field. He is described in the patent as "Clement Sysley of Barrowhall in Essex, gentleman, son of Francis, son of Charles Sysley of Founteynes in Yorkshire, gentleman, who was the son of Christopher, son of Francis Sysley of Founteynes, gentleman." Sisley must have made the place his home, for in his will* he bequeathed " the gownes, pykes, crossbows and other weapons to Thos. Sysley to go with the house, and to remain as standards for ever in Eastbury Hall." According to Lysons† Thomas Sisley sold the house before 1608 to Augustine Steward, and he gives the following sequence of owners:—In 1628 Martin Steward sold it to Jacob Price; in 1646 it passed from George Price to William Knightley, whose widow in 1650 conveyed it to the well-known Sir Thomas Vyner, Lord Mayor of London in 1653-4, who perhaps made it his country residence before purchasing the old mansion near the church at Hackney. In 1714 his representatives sold it to William Browne, from whose nephew, William Sedgewick, it came into the hands of John Weldale in 1740. According to Morant, writing in 1768, it then belonged " to two or three sisters of the name of Weldon (sic), and they also have some portion of the tithes here." They were presumably daughters of John Weldale, and in 1773 Ann Weldale, the last survivor, left it to Mary, wife of the Rev. Wasey Sterry, with remainder to her issue. When Lysons wrote in 1796 it was the joint property of her sons Wasey Sterry of Rumford and his brothers Thomas and Henry Sterry. We are told in a footnote that " the whole descent of this manor" was " taken from title deeds obligingly communicated" by the first named, who according to Black‡ was in his time " yet the proprietor of Eastbury and of the rectorial tithes of 1,200 acres in its neighbourhood." He adds the following statement: " For almost a hundred years it hath been occupied by lessees and thereby degraded into a farmhouse." Three Thomas Newmans, grandfather, father and son, "successively occupied it until 1792, when the third of that name left it, and dying was buried at Barking. The next occupiers were Mr. Brushfield, mentioned by Lysons in 1796, and Mr. Scott,§ farmers, in whose time the house was neglected so much that ever since its ruin has been hastening."

The evil days on which the house had fallen may be further illustrated by quotations from W. H. Black's account in 1834 of the building. "At the time of the riots in 1780," he says, "the figures that stood in

---

* *Quoted by Cutts, " Proceedings Essex Arch. Soc.," Old Series, Vol. II., page* 138.
† " *Environs of London* " (1796), *Vol. IV., page* 77.
‡ " *Eastbury, Illustrated, etc.*," T. H. Clarke and W. H. Black, 1834.
§ *In the supplementary volume to Lysons'* " *Environs of London* " (1811) *the name of the tenant is given as William Scott.*

the garden wall* were taken down by Mrs Scott's order and thrown in the pond." Of the building itself he tells us that "four of the chimney-pieces were lately bought by the Rev. Thomas Fanshawe, who preserves them in the vicarage house at Parsloes in Dagenham parish. Moreover, the fine oak floors have been taken up to repair the barns, timbers have been torn away for like purposes, and even one of the towers have been pulled down for its materials Besides the kitchen, two rooms only are occupied by as many workmen and their wives, one of which has but lately been fitted up for that purpose, they are employed by the present farmers Thomas and Edward George Pollet, who live at Dagenham and hold the house and about 65 acres of land on a lease from Mr Sterry" James Thorne,† writing in 1876, states that the house "had become almost a ruin, but has been restored by the present owner."

A brief reference must be made to the tradition that Eastbury was connected with the Gunpowder Plot, which occurred at the time of its possession by the Sisley family Lysons‡ says, "There is a tradition relating to this house, either, as some say, that the conspirators who concerted the Gunpowder Plot held their meetings there, or as others, that it was the residence of Lord Monteagle when he received the letter that led to its discovery, both, perhaps, equally devoid of foundation. The latter is more probable, though there is no other corroboration of it than that Lord Monteagle lived in the parish about the time, as appears by the register of baptisms" C R B Barrett§ gives a variation of the former tradition in the local belief that from the summit of the tower the conspirators hoped to see the flash and hear the report announcing the accomplishment of their design. The only support for this story lies in the deposition of a fisherman of Barking that Guido Fawkes had hired a Barking boat to take him and another man to Gravelines and bring them back

As regards the supposed connection of William Parker, fourth Baron Monteagle, with the house, Streatfeild,‖ quoting from Mr. King's contribution to the second of the Essex Archæological Society's volumes, gives the following extract from the parish registers of Barking, with unimportant errors, which are here corrected —"1607, William, the sonne of Sir William Parker, Knighte, Lord Monteagle, baptised the

---

* See page 29 for a further reference to the niches in the garden wall The mention of Mrs. Scott does not agree with his statements regarding the occupation of the Newmans until 1792, unless the house was divided
† "Handbook to the Environs of London"
‡ "Environs of London"
§ "Essex Highways and Byways."
‖ R I B A. Transactions, 1871–2

third day of December." He thus shows that Lord Monteagle was residing in the neighbourhood, but he goes too far when he assumes that Lord Monteagle rented Eastbury "from the owner, Mr. Steward, who it is known did not reside at Eastbury but in the parish of St. Sepulchre, where he afterwards died." There is no evidence that Sisley had parted with the house to Steward as early as 1605, although it seems probable that the place was occupied by tenants during the latter's ownership, if only from the presence of the arms of the More family which appears in the paintings above the hall that date from this period. The suggestion that Lord Monteagle received the notorious letter, warning him of danger, at Barking is disposed of by his own evidence that it was at his house in Hoxton that it was put into the hands of his footman " whom he had sent on an errand over the street."

P. N.

WROUGHT-IRON HANDLE AND HINGE.

ARCHITECTURAL DESCRIPTION.

A LARGE part of Essex has escaped the modern passion for change, and to this is due her richness in unrestored and unspoiled buildings of a past age. The charm of Eastbury House lies in the fact that it remains practically untouched by the sinister hands of "improvement," and at least externally is able to show us to-day the actual craftsmanship of its sixteenth-century builder.

The exact date of the building or who erected it is unknown. Several writers have inferred from the history of its ownership that it was built by Clement Sisley, who held the property in 1557, and in whose family it remained until about 1607. "There is a tradition," says Black,* "of the date 1572 having been cut in brickwork in some part of the hall, destroyed many years ago by a person who dwelt there," and he adds that in Philip Luckmore's "Tablet of Memories" † is "Eastbury House, Essex, built 1572." In Grose's "Antiquities"—the edition the preface of which is dated 1787—we are told there was a date 1573 on a leaden spout on the south side of the house, and this, together with the date in the hall, has been referred to by subsequent writers. *Date of the building*

Apart from this date, which if confirmed would not necessarily be the date of the house, the building itself gives very little evidence of belonging to the Elizabethan period. It is true that the symmetrical disposition of the plan in the form of the letter H and the regular grouping of the gables show the influence of the Renaissance and give a character in keeping with the domestic architecture of Elizabeth's reign. On the other hand, there is a striking absence of Renaissance details. The finials to the gables, the moulded chimney-stacks, the traceried pediment over the porch, and the stone chimney-pieces, all show late Gothic or Tudor forms. The two circular newel stairs suggest a date earlier than the introduction of the square Elizabethan staircases, and the arrangement of the hall is, of course, not inconsistent with its late mediæval appearance. In the absence of any documentary evidence it is perhaps enough to say that the house may possibly have been built before the dissolution of Barking Abbey, and that, if it should prove to have been the work of an owner after the Reformation, it shows an unusual conservatism and devotion to traditional features.

After these introductory remarks we can proceed to a description of the various parts of the building. Its plan (Plate 3) has already been referred to as in form like the letter H, the main block lying east and *The plan*

---

* "*Eastbury, Illustrated by Elevations, Plans, Sections, Views, etc.*," by Thomas Hutchings Clarke, with a historical sketch by William Henry Black. London, 1834.
† Eighth edition, 1792. 12mo. Page 222.

d

19

west and comprising the hall and rooms above, the two wings projecting slightly forwards to the north, and with greater depth to the south, where an enclosed courtyard is formed by the building on three sides and a high wall on the fourth. There are three storeys with a cellar under the west wing. On the north side a square three-storeyed porch adjoins the west wing, and two lofty staircase turrets, roughly octagonal without and circular within, are attached to the hall in the angles of the courtyard. There are three fine brick chimney-stacks in the courtyard and others rise from the roofs, having well-designed, moulded set-offs and grouped octagonal shafts with moulded caps and bases.

The walls are built of red brick in English bond and are of fine material and workmanship. Moulded bricks are used in the plinth, the jambs,

PLAN BY P. J. MARVIN.

mullions, transoms, and labels of the windows, the gables, the entrance porch, and the corbels and shafts of the chimney-stacks. The eastern stair turret—the only considerable feature of the house which has been demolished*—still shows a fine handrail of moulded brick cut in the remaining wall. A diagonal arrangement of bricks with dark headers is to be seen externally, and this, together with the size of the bricks (10 ins. by 4½ ins. by 2½ ins.), agrees with the brickwork to be found in Essex in the early part of the sixteenth century. Another local feature is the cement covering to the brick windows, worked to represent quoins on either side (and to the stairturrets), which conforms with a practice now recognised as having been widely in vogue in this county. The roofs are tiled.

* See also page 17. The tower is shown in a drawing in Ogborne's "History of Essex," but was pulled down before the publication of the book in 1814.

20

The majority of the windows on all floors are of six lights, three above and three below the transom, which is of brick, hollow-chamfered on both sides, as are also the jambs and mullions. The north front (Plate 6) has two pairs in each wing, one to each of the ground and first floors and one window in the gable. The hall has three windows, with three above (now blocked up) on the first floor, and two on the second floor, each in a small gable. The porch (Plates 9 and 10) has moulded brick jambs, and a four-centred arch in a square label surmounted by a brick pediment with tracery, and three finials covered with a pattern in cut brick. The rooms over the porch have two windows on each floor, one facing north and one east, each of four lights, two above and two below the transom. The gables have panelled angle finials, set obliquely, and hexagonal ones at the apex, carried on moulded corbels. They originally rose some height above the parapet, but the moulded bases of the upper portions alone remain. The east elevation (Plate 8), which overlooks the walled garden, has a gable at each end with a smaller one in the centre, having windows like those to the north. The first floor has a row of seven windows, which are repeated on the ground floor, except that one light of the central window has to give place to the garden entrance, an oak door in a heavy square frame. The west elevation is similar to the east and is only varied by a modern porch to the kitchen.

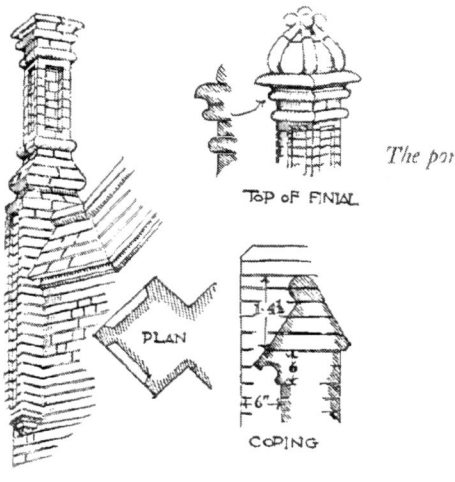

The courtyard to the south (Plate 7) presents the most picturesque aspect of all the views of the house, the gables, lofty chimney-stacks, and the remaining staircase turret being grouped together to form a skyline of quiet, unusual beauty. The gables of the two wings are similar to those on the north side, except that there is one window only on each floor and a single opening above the top window to give light to the roof. The wings are connected by a wall some 13 feet in height with a somewhat decayed square-headed door in the centre. On the inner side of each wing and flush with the wall is a small two-storied projection containing the *guardrobes*, an early feature. The eastern face of the west wing has no windows, but in the centre is the (kitchen) chimney-stack, which projects boldly from the wall

(Plate 21), and is increased in width by two corbels of moulded brickwork as far as the first floor, when by a series of set-offs it reaches the base of its three octagonal shafts. This stack adjoins the staircase turret, which on its eastern face has five storeys, occupied at the base by a square-framed batten door (Plate 23) and four single-light windows above. On its south-eastern side it also has four windows, each in a correspondingly lower position than the others, except the top one, which forms part of a series of seven windows,* making an octagonal lantern at the top of the tower. Cement quoins mark the ingles of the stair, and below the lantern is a moulded course of brickwork. The parapet was originally adorned with little cylindrical carved finials at the angles.

Hall chimney-stack — The greater part of the space on the south wall of the main building between this stair and the eastern turret, which is now missing, is occupied by the (hall) chimney-stack, with its five flues and corresponding shafts, which are here octagonal with hollow sides. A small space to the west of the stack leaves room for a four-light window (two lights above and two below the transom) to both the ground and first floors. A similar window on the ground floor occurs to the east, but over it is turned a segmental arch (Plate 21) on two moulded corbels, to carry a part of the chimney-stack, which is here slightly recessed from the main face. The angles of the stack are chamfered at the ground floor level to admit more light to the windows. The west face of the east wing has a central chimney-stack with three shafts, of which the bases alone remain. Between the stacks and the demolished stair are two windows similar to those just described on the south wall of the main building, one to each floor.

Entrance door — The original internal arrangements of the house have been considerably altered and practically all the fittings have disappeared. The porch once had a fine oak door, with wrought-iron knocker (illustrations of which have been preserved, see Plate 10 and page 12), and leads into the hall behind the screen. W. H. Black† refers to the "passage under the gallery of the hall, which was entered on the left hand through a screen, whereof only the posts and bressummer now remain." These have long ago given way to a modern partition; it

The hall — is very doubtful if there was ever a gallery, as the height of the hall would not admit of this. Black further describes two doors communicating from the screen passage to the kitchen wing, which would conform to the usage of the time. Another interesting note of his refers the reader to T. H. Clarke's plan, which "shows where the hall was paved with black slates (16 inches square), the other parts were paved with small red tiles, except the dais, which was floored"

* *There is no window on the south face, as it is blocked by the chimney-stack.*
† "*Eastbury, Illustrated, etc.*," 1834.

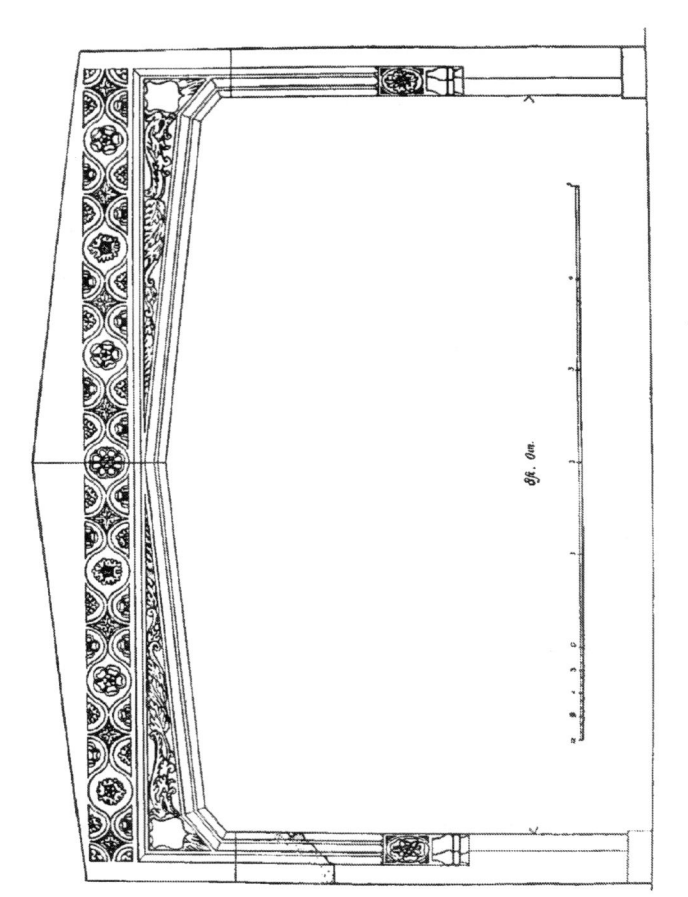

FIREPLACE, FORMERLY IN HALL.

(Plate 3). The paved floor and dais have both disappeared, and the fine stone fireplace, of which a drawing is reproduced, was removed to Parsloes but is no longer there. The room is now divided into two and entirely modernised, but originally it must have been a fine room, 40 feet by 21 feet, with its screen and fireplace, its three windows to the north and two to the south, and with its appropriate decorations. At the east end towards the passage, which gave entrance to the principal stairs, the parlours, and the entrance to the walled garden, is a wide recess, which Black describes as " containing an iron shelf raised on a brick arch and seemingly used as a sideboard "

The passage to the garden is 9 ft 2 ins wide The two doors of the hall (now blocked) and principal stair respectively occupy the west end, *Garden door* while to the east is the garden door flanked on each side by one light of the adjoining windows (Plate 25) The original oak door, hung to a heavy chamfered frame, remains . we have already remarked that by its position it cuts into one of the windows under the side transom light It is interesting that the remaining lights of the two side windows are backed by the thickness of the wall, and have been introduced for reasons of symmetry alone On each side of the passage are doors, now blocked, leading into the parlours, that to the south being a room of some 32 feet by 20 feet, now used as a stable The fireplace is bricked up and a modern entrance has been cut through the south wall beneath the window, which has been removed and replaced by a small light, the original brick label alone remaining The north parlour is rather over 25 feet long, with the same width as the other, and is divided into two out-houses, a large modern cartway having been made in the east wall in place of the northernmost window and another modern doorway at the southern end of the same wall. The fireplace has been removed, but Mr Black's drawing of it is here shown

The rooms in the west wing are approached from the hall by two modern doors in the wall behind the screen These give on a room *The west* some 20 feet square at the north end, and a passage room, about 8 feet *wing* wide, from which the second staircase and the kitchen were entered The door to the stair is now bricked up A long recess occupies the western half of the north wall of this passage room, and to the right of it was a curious recess, not unlike a piscina, with a cusped and foliated arch of fourteenth or fifteenth century character. This niche was discovered and recorded by Mr. Robert Pearsall in 1872, and he has suggested that it marked the position of a chapel It is improbable, however, that it would have been placed in the western and kitchen wing, and its Gothic character would suggest that it had been inserted for some reason from an earlier building

Panelled The kitchen with the large fireplace in its eastern wall has been modern-
room ised, but at the north end of this wing is a small room 20 feet by

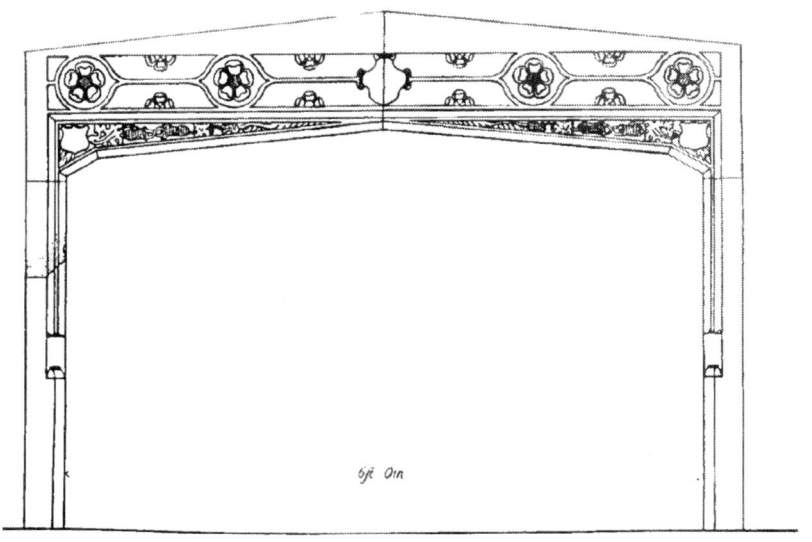

FIREPLACE FORMERLY IN N.E. ROOM, GROUND FLOOR.

14 feet, the walls of which are covered from floor to ceiling by sixteenth century oak panelling with moulded frames (Plates 14 and 26). The floor of this and the south room are raised over low cellars and approached by a few stairs.

The first floor is now inhabited only in the west wing, which has been modernised within and possesses no ancient features. Over the old hall were originally two rooms with fireplaces (now bricked up) in the central chimney-stack. The eastern room has plastered walls on which remain traces of elaborate painted decoration dating from the late sixteenth or early seventeenth century. A scale drawing of the painting on the partition, which has now disappeared, is reproduced among T. H. Clarke's drawings of the house* (Plate 30). The scheme of decoration can still be seen, and consists of a series of arched panels separated by twin columns of spiral shape, with foliated pedestals and capitals apparently coloured to represent stone. The line of columns and arches stands on a panelled plinth, with moulded base and cornice, while above at ceiling level runs an entablature with a triglyph over each column. The plinth or dado is panelled, having classical busts depicted in the panels beneath each column. The whole is drawn in a rough perspective, and the arched spaces between the columns

The first floor
Paintings

* "*Eastbury, Illustrated, etc.*," 1834.

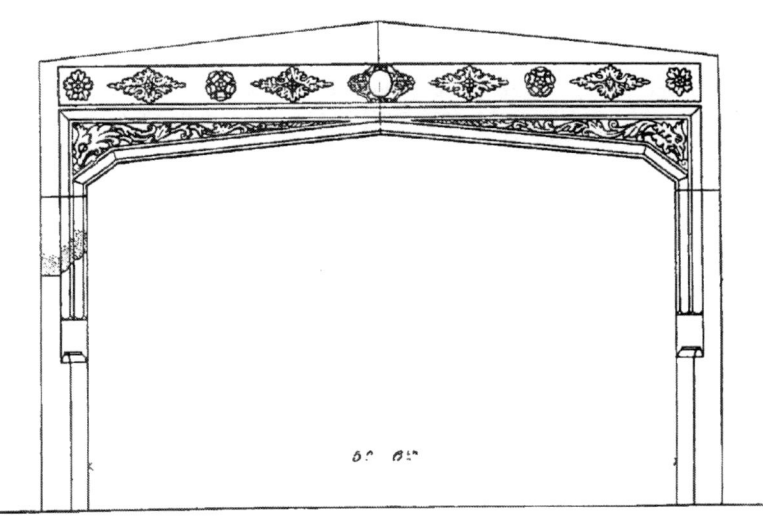

FIREPLACE FORMERLY IN PAINTED ROOM OVER HALL.

represent openings or windows through which one looks upon a seascape with fishing vessels of various types in bright natural colours. The east and west walls were treated alike, each with a plain square-headed doorway on the right-hand side, over which was a panel of painted strapwork ornament, and the remainder of the wall arranged in three bays as described above. The south wall had a fireplace in the centre (now removed), over which was a double-arched opening with a pendant under the spandrel, bearing a coat of arms :—*Ermine between six cocks a fess Gules.* This is the coat of More (co. Chester), but its owner has not been identified. The opening here shows a landscape, Dutch in character, with an avenue of trees and a town in the distance, with towers and spires. The fireplace was flanked by a single painted column and a window with seascape on each side as on the other walls. The columns between the windows on the north side can still be traced.

More (Chester)

From the western room a door leads into a small room over the porch, where is a trap door opening on a space some 3 ft. 6 ins. deep between the floor of the room and the ceiling of the porch below. This space is lighted by a loophole in the eastern wall.

The long gallery

The east wing on the first floor, overlooking the walled-in garden, was probably designed as the long gallery, although this may have been on the second floor. The entrance from the painted room and now demolished staircase is bricked up, and the present approach is by wooden steps from the stable below. A part of the room at the south end is partitioned off, but the framework is not original. There were two fireplaces in the gallery, on the west wall, but the southernmost alone remains in its place (Plates 13 and 27). It is of freestone with moulded jambs and a flat pointed arch, the shoulders being obliquely cut in a straight line instead of rounded. This form, which is not uncommon in the Tudor period, was followed in all the fireplaces in the house. The spandrels have small shields and foliage, and a stone frieze of alternate circles and lozenges filled with roses and leafage extends over the arch. The original brick-lined opening with a panel of herring-bone work at the back remains.

The second floor is now open to the roof (Plate 28), the plaster ceilings having been removed and the floor boards taken from the joists. The timbers are in a fine state of preservation, and the roof presents a picturesque appearance with its queen-posts, tie-beams, and rafters all revealed. The constructional parts of the floor have been removed over the painted room and over the long gallery. There is only one fireplace

FIREPLACE FORMERLY IN WEST ROOM OVER HALL.

on the second floor, a simple three-centred arch of chamfered brickwork set in the central stack above the hall.

The walls of the east wing on this floor still exhibit traces of painting, the subjects of which were figures in costume, some of which have been drawn by T. H. Clarke (Plate 32) and Elizabeth Ogborne, and are reproduced here. The prevailing colour used was apparently a shade of green.

The original oak door from the staircase to the west wing is still in its place. The stair is of massive oak, with a central newel and solid treads. It rises to a stage above the second floor, where the windows in seven sides of the octagon give fine views over the flat country. A trap door leads to the lead roof over the stair, whence a fine view (Plate 24) of the old tiled roofs and lofty chimney shafts is obtained.

The eastern wing of the house looks out on a square walled garden, some 100 feet square, now used for vegetables, but " where," in 1834, " the box plants have grown rank and high."* The original sixteenth-century walls are still largely intact, having a brick chamfered plinth and coping. On the east side are four niches, and two on the south wall, with triangular-shaped heads, formed by two sloping bricks. The openings are 18 inches in height and 11 inches wide, the depth also being 11 inches. There has been some speculation on the purpose of these niches, which occur not infrequently in the garden walls of sixteenth-century houses. Those discovered some

PAINTED FIGURES IN GALLERY (SECOND FLOOR).

years ago at Bromley in Kent are almost identical but somewhat larger. We have seen that in 1780 these niches held figures,† which may, of course, have been the original garden ornaments. It is suggested that

* W. H. Black in " Eastbury Illustrated, etc.," 1834.
† See page 17.

they were formed to hold lanterns, or even cages for birds, such as Bacon in his "Essay of Gardens" describes in hedges "framed upon Carpenter's work." In some parts of the country similar recesses were used for bees, but those at Eastbury are small for this purpose and may simply have been intended for hanging plants. Black (1834) states that an orchard adjoined the garden, "where some old fruit trees yet stand," and it was approached no doubt by the gateway in the east wall, the opening of which has been enlarged in modern times
The south and west walls of a second square garden remain on the west side of the house
Of the outbuildings two original barns are left, to the south-west of the main building The smaller adjoins the west garden, and has a west porch and a short aisle to the north. The larger barn (Plate 29) stands some distance from the house and measures 95 feet by 40 feet. It is divided into three aisles by massive oak uprights, and is five bays long, with a half bay at each end and a porch to the east Originally thatched, it is now roofed with corrugated iron, but most of the original timbers remain, except the external weather-boarding, which is modern
To the south of the house is a pond, and there are a number of trees around the building.

W H G

APPENDIX
BIBLIOGRAPHICAL REFERENCES

1740. The History and Antiquities of Essex, from the Collections of T Jekyll By N Salmon, p 21

1780. Antiquities of England and Wales By Francis Grose. Vol I pp. 122-123. (With engraving)

1796 Environs of London By Rev Daniel Lysons Vol IV. (With engraving of House)

1803 Beauties of England and Wales By E. W Brayley and J Britton Vol V , pp 462-463

1814 History of Essex By Elizabeth Ogborne, pp. 48-49 (With engravings)

1816 History and Antiquities of Essex By P Morant Vol I Hundred of Becontree, p 5

1818 Excursions in the County of Essex Vol I , p 181

1819 Ditto ditto Another edition Vol I , p 204

1822 Paterson's Roads By Edward Mogg, p 334

1823 Pencil sketch in the British Museum J. C Buckler

1833 Domestic Architecture of the Reigns of Elizabeth and James I By T H Clarke (Plate XIX and title-page)

1834 Eastbury Illustrated by elevations, plans, sections, views and other delineations by Thomas Hutchings Clarke With a historical sketch by William Henry Black Quarto

1848. History and Gazetteer of Essex By William White, p. 216.

1861 People's History of Essex By W D Coller, pp 464-465.

1863 Transactions Essex Archæological Society, 1st Ser , Vol II . pp 134-138 By Rev E L Cutts

1871 Transactions Royal Institute of British Architects, 1871-2 T E C Streatfeild, pp 165-172 (With plan and sketch.)

1872. Architectural Association Sketch Book, 1871-2 (North elevation of house, drawn by H. Avern)

1880. The Builder (4th September, 1880), p 301 (Drawing of courtyard and ground-plan of house, by Edward Clarke.)

1887 Durrant's Handbook for Essex. Written by Miller Christy, p 41

1896 Notes and Queries, 8th Series, Vol X , pp 552-3 Notes by Thomas Bird, H G Griffinhoope and Edward H Marshall

1897 Notes and Queries, 8th Series, Vol XI pp 37-38 Note by Francis Sterry
1902 Home Counties Magazine, Vol IV (Photograph opposite p 146)
1902. East London Antiquities Ed by Walter A Locks (J.T. Page), p. 173
1903 Architectural Association Sketch Book, 3rd Ser, Vol VII, 1903 Five drawings by P J Marvin, viz —
    1 Plan
    2 North elevation.
    3. East and west elevation
    4 Details
    5 View of south front
1905. Picturesque Essex By R H E Hill Sketches by Duncan Moul, pp. 137-138. (With illustrations on p. 135)
1909. Little Guide to Essex J C Cox, pp 92-93
1909. The Domestic Architecture of England during the Tudor period. By Thomas Garner and Arthur Stratton, Vol 2, Text, pp 138-140 (four illustrations), also fig 297 (brickwork) on p 213 of text
    Plate LXXXV   North elevation and details
    Plate CLXVI   Chimney-piece.
    Plate CLXXV   Door
1911 A History of Architecture in London By Walter H. Godfrey, pp 143, 164, 174, 175, and Figs 122, 123
1915 The Building News, 30th April and 4th June Drawings by Hubert V C Curtis
not dated Greater London By Edward Walford, Vol I, p 524 With engraving (on p 522) after Lysons

In the *Earle Collection of Essex Views* in the Library of the Society of Antiquaries of London are the following —

1780 Engraving of South view of house, "Sparrow &c" 5¼ inches by 4½ inches (From Grose's "Antiquities")
1796 Engraving of South view of house. 7¾ inches by 6¾ inches. (From Lysons' "Environs")
1814 Engraving of South view of house, and also view of three figures (two musicians and one soldier) on one plate (from Ogborne's "History of Essex").
1816 Pencil drawing of house, 6½ inches by 5 inches Aug 1816

1818 Engraving of house, $3\frac{3}{8}$ inches by $2\frac{3}{8}$ inches. Drawn by W Deeble, engraved by J Hawksworth (From "Excursions in the County of Essex")

1860 Lithograph of house, 9 inches by 4 inches 'K F, sketched 1860"

not dated Engraving of South view of house, $3\frac{1}{2}$ inches by $2\frac{3}{8}$ inches. Drawn by W Deeble, engraved by J Greig (From the "Antiquarian Itinerary")

not dated Engraving of South view of house, $6\frac{3}{8}$ inches by $3\frac{7}{8}$ inches. Drawn by W Bartlett, engraved by W Watkins

In the *Phené Spiers Collection* at the Victoria and Albert Museum are six sheets of measured drawings, dated 1871, by Walter L Spiers (ref D 289–294)

In the MS records of the *Royal Commission on Historical Monuments (England)* are photographs of the building (1914) and the Commissioners' report

The *London Survey Committee's Collection* includes a number of Photographs besides those reproduced in the present volume

INDEX.

	page
Abbott, Margery	15
Abbott, William	15
Allhallows, Barking	14
Barking Abbey	13
Barking, parish of	13
Barrowhall, Essex	16
Becontree, hundred of	13
Breame, Arthur	15
Browne, William	16
Brushfield, —	16
Coleman Street Ward	14
Dagenham, Essex	13, 17
Denham, Elizabeth	13, 14, 15
Denham, Nicholas	13, 15
Denham, Sir William	13, 14, 15
Eastbury, Manor of	13
Fanshawe, Rev Thomas	17
Fawkes, Guido	17
Founteynes, Yorkshire	16
Grocers' Company, The	14, 15
Ironmongers' Company, The	14, 15
Keele, John	15
Knightley, William	16
Lyston, Devonshire	13, 15

	page
Monteagle, Lord, *see* Parker	
More (Chester), Arms of	- 26
Newman, Thomas	- 16
Parker, William, Lord Monteag'e	17, 18
Parsloes	- 17
Pollet, Edward George	- 17
Pollet, Thomas	- 17
Price, George	- 16
Price, Jacob	- 16
Rippleside	- 13
St Mary Staining	13, 15
St Olave Jewry	13, 15
Scott, William	- 16
Sedgewick, William	- 16
Sisley, Charles	- 16
Sisley, Christopher	- 16
Sisley, Clement	15, 16
Sisley, Francis	- 16
Sisley, Thomas	- 16
Sterry, Henry	- 16
Sterry, Mary	- 16
Sterry, Thomas	- 16
Sterry, Rev. Wasey	- 16
Steward, Augustine	- 16
Steward, Martin	- 16
Vyner, Sir Thomas	- 16
Weldale, Ann	- 16
Weldale, John	- 16
Westbury, Manor of	13, 14

34

HERE ENDS THE ELEVENTH MONOGRAPH OF THE
LONDON SURVEY COMMITTEE ON EASTBURY MANOR
HOUSE, BARKING, WHICH WAS WRITTEN IN 1917, AND
PRINTED FOR THE COMMITTEE BY MESSRS. EYRE AND
SPOTTISWOODE, LIMITED, EAST HARDING STREET, E.C.
MDCCCCXVII.

Published in England by the London Survey Committee, 27, Abingdon Street, Westminster, S.W.
600 copies, of which this is No.307

PLATE 2

Eastbury Manor House,
Barking, Essex. 1572.

PLATE 3

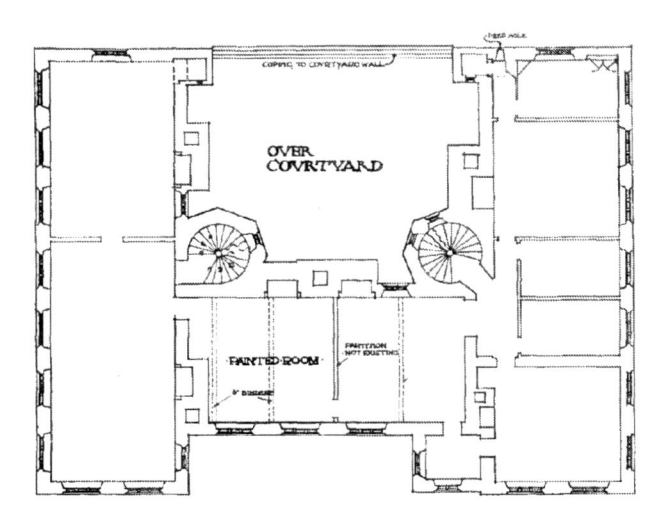

FIRST FLOOR PLAN

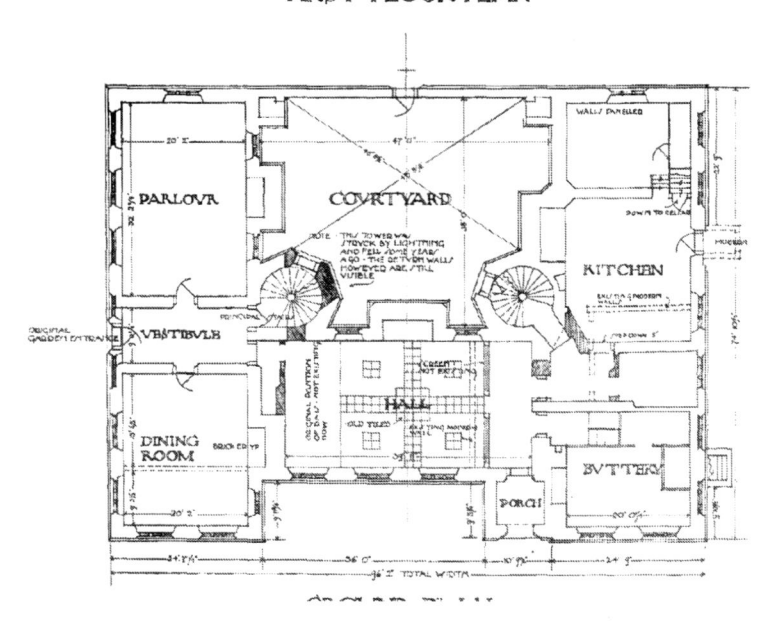

PLATE 4

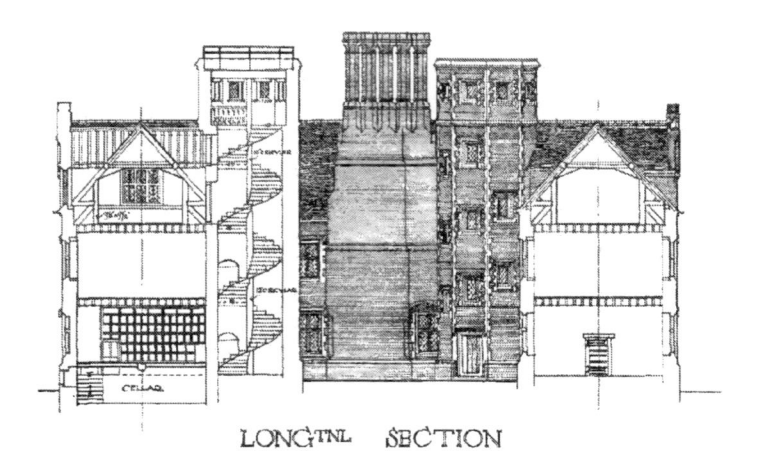

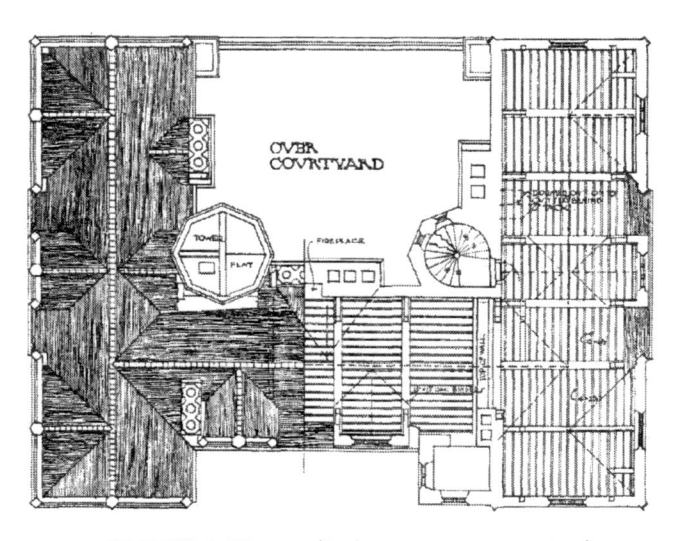

LONG^{TNL} SECTION

PART ROOF AND SECOND FLOOR PLANS

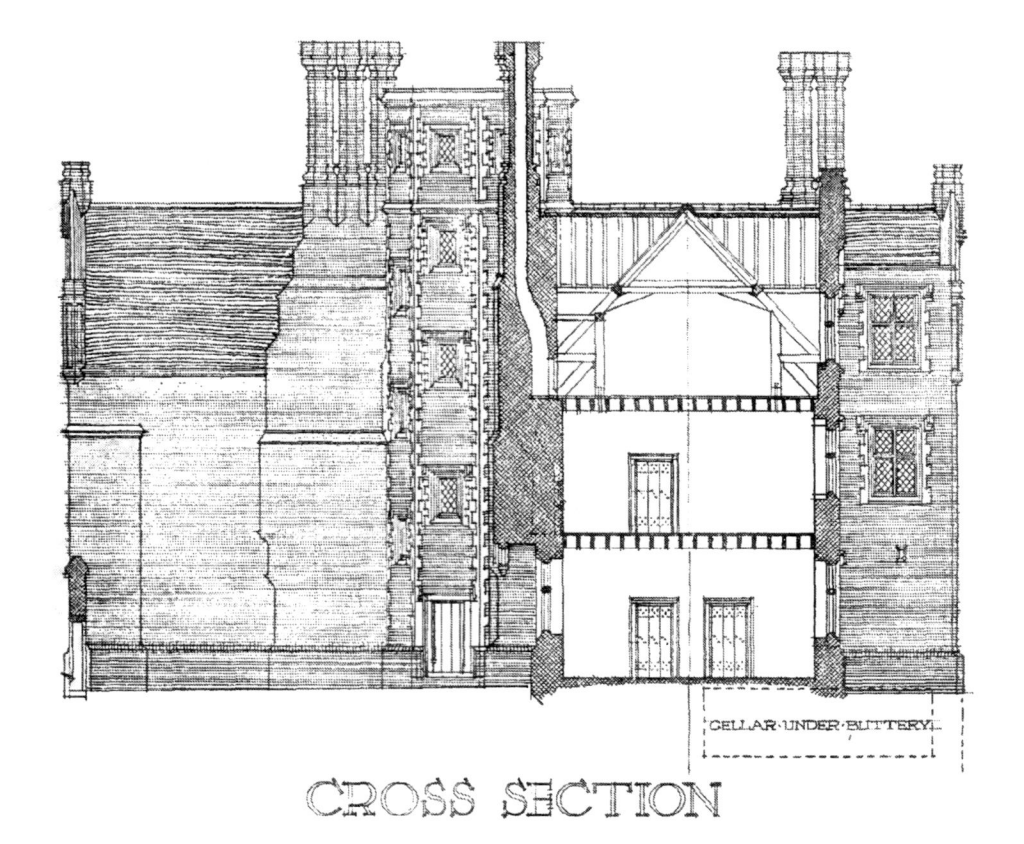

PLATE 5

CROSS SECTION

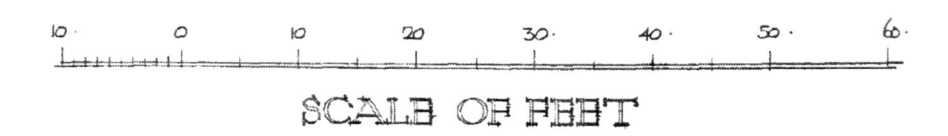

CELLAR·UNDER·BUTTERY

SCALE OF FEET

PLATE 6

NORTH ELEVATION

SCALE OF FEET

PLATE 7

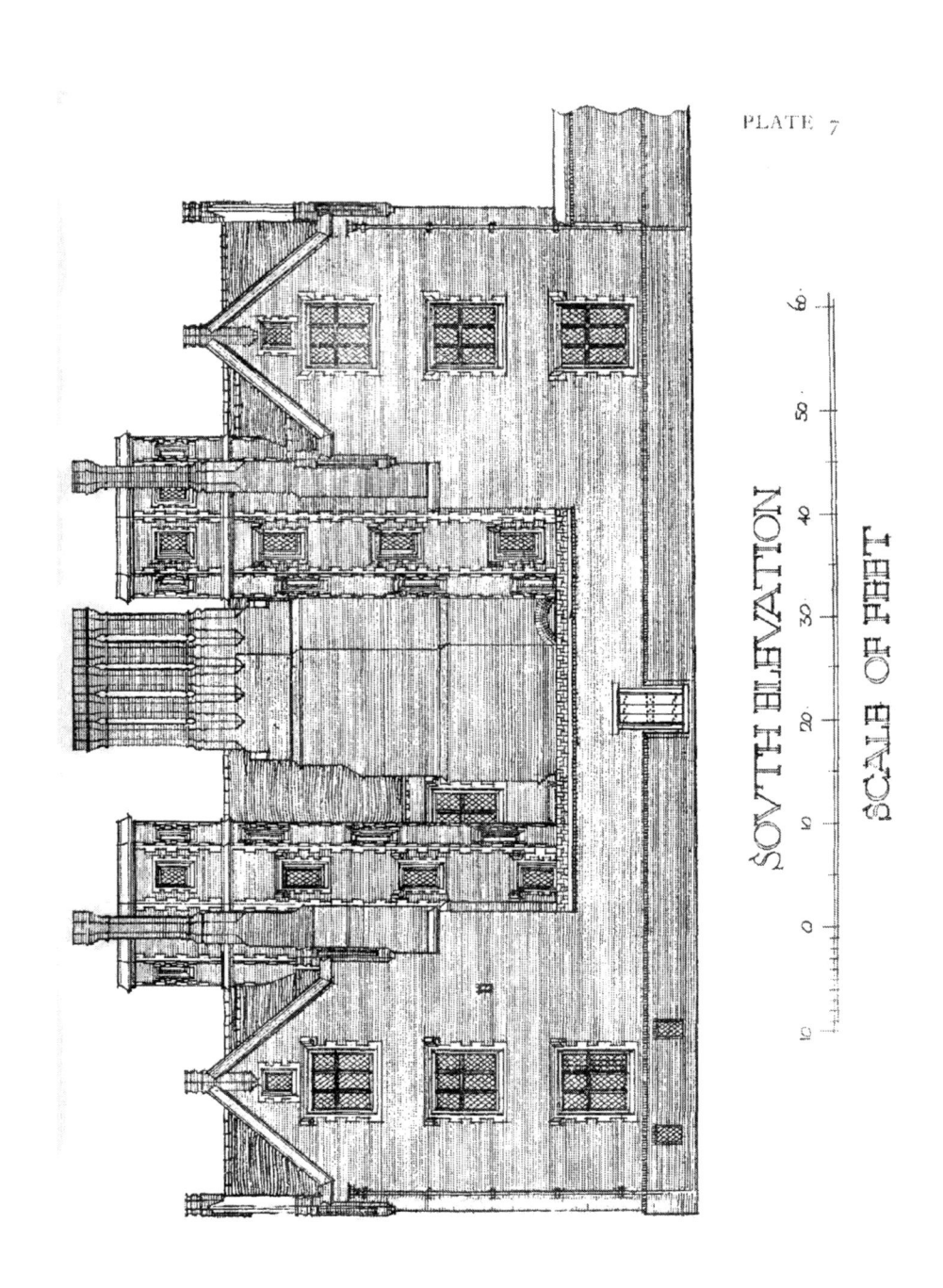

SOUTH ELEVATION

SCALE OF FEET

PLATE 8

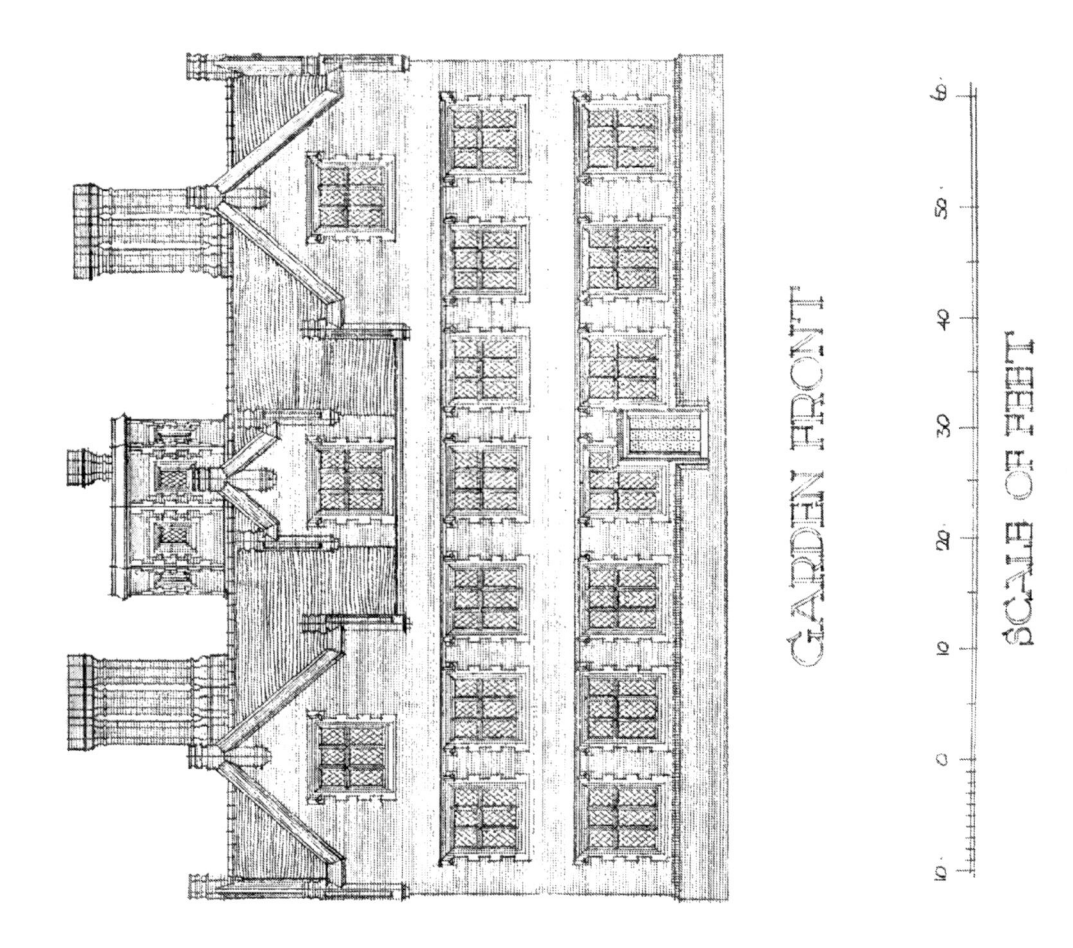

GARDEN FRONT

SCALE OF FEET

EASTBURY HOUSE
DETAIL OF PART OF
NORTH ELEVATION

SCALE OF FEET

PLATE 9

PLATE 10

PORCH AND ENTRANCE DOOR
Drawn by T. H. CLARKE

EASTBURY
HOUSE

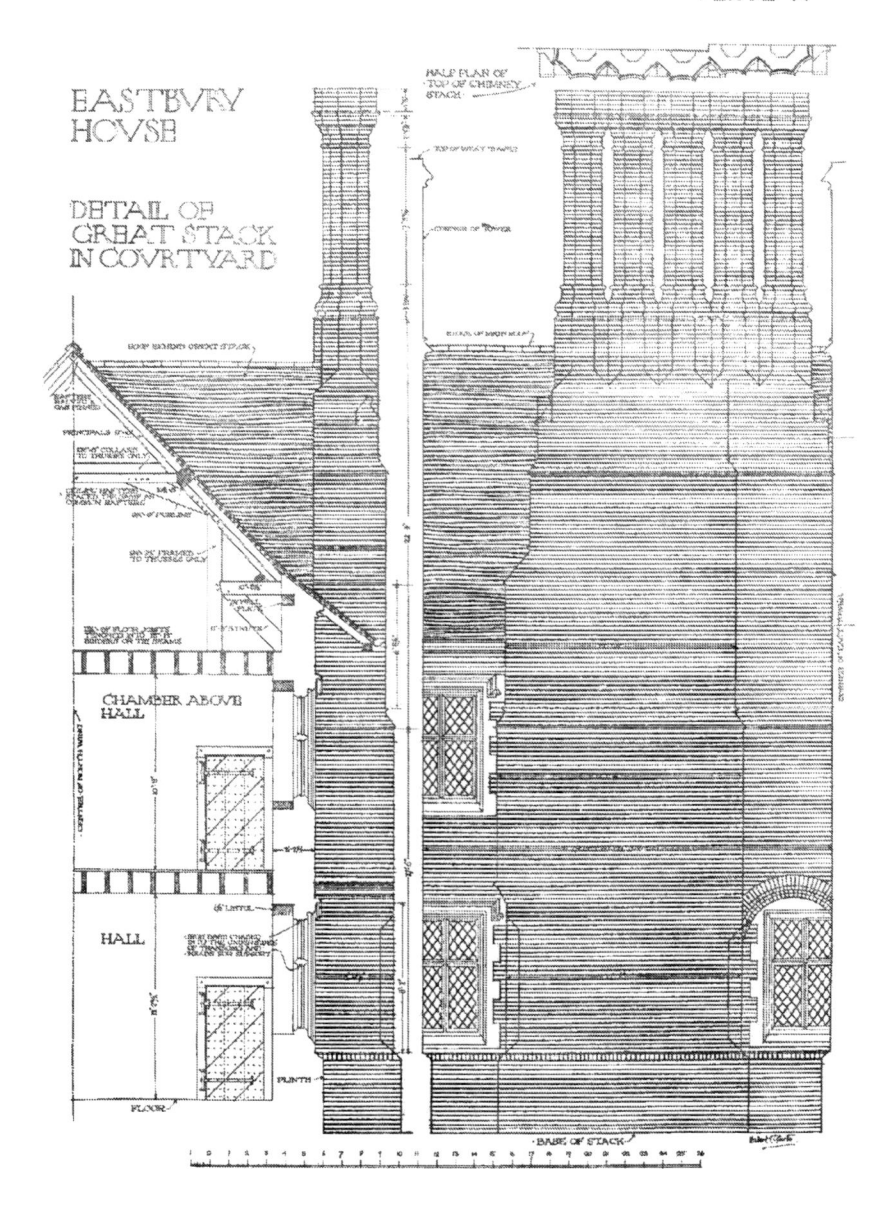

DETAIL OF
GREAT STACK
IN COURTYARD

PLATE 12

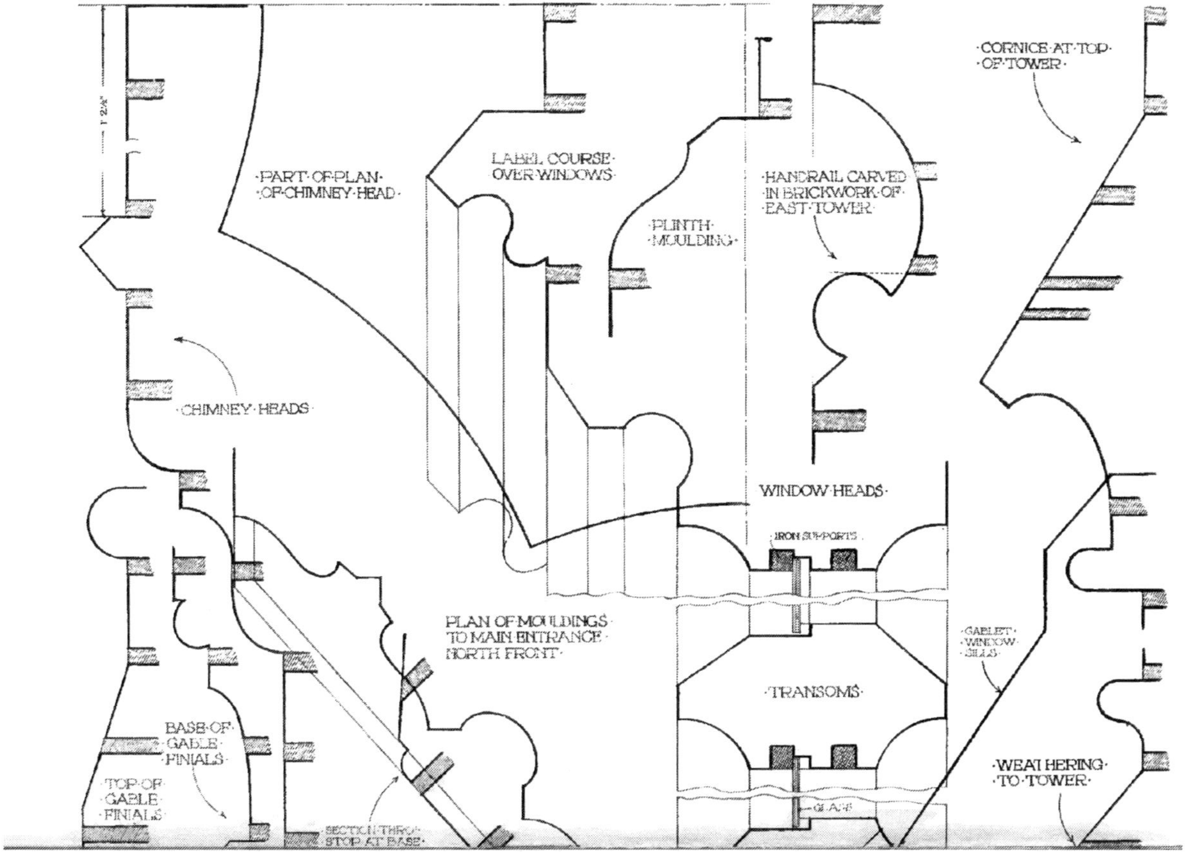
1' 2¼"
·PART·OF·PLAN·
·OF·CHIMNEY·HEAD·
LABEL·COURSE·
OVER·WINDOWS·
·PLINTH·
·MOULDING·
·HANDRAIL·CARVED·
·IN·BRICKWORK·OF·
·EAST·TOWER·
·CORNICE·AT·TOP·
·OF·TOWER·
·CHIMNEY·HEADS·
·WINDOW·HEADS·
·IRON·SUPPORTS·
PLAN·OF·MOULDINGS·
TO·MAIN·ENTRANCE·
NORTH·FRONT·
·TRANSOMS·
·GLASS·
·GABLET·
·WINDOW·
·SILLS·
BASE·OF·
GABLE·
FINIALS·
·TOP·OF·
GABLE·
FINIALS·
·SECTION·THRO·
STOP·AT·BASE·
·WEATHERING·
·TO·TOWER·

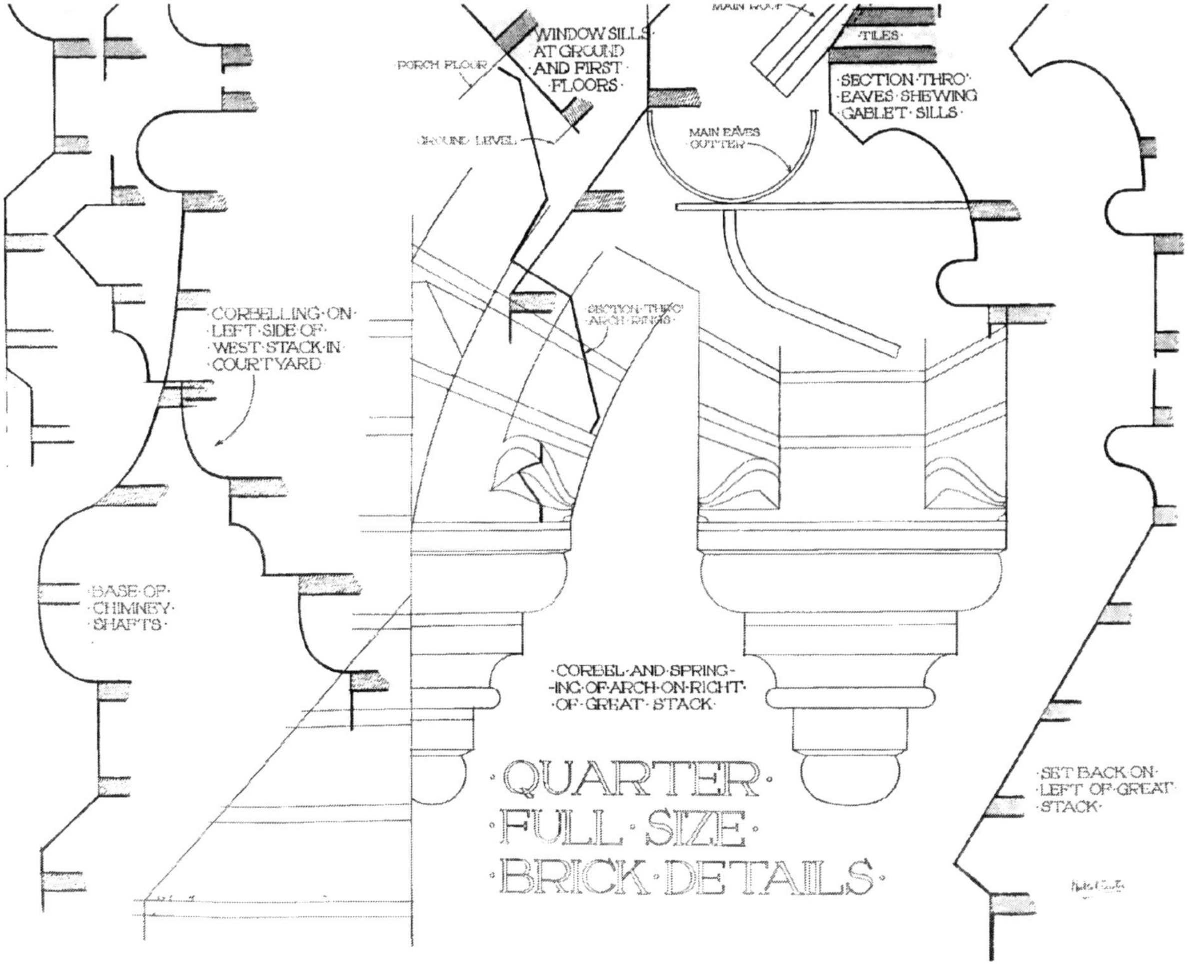

MAIN ROOF
TILES
WINDOW SILLS AT GROUND AND FIRST FLOORS
PORCH FLOOR
GROUND LEVEL
MAIN EAVES GUTTER
SECTION·THRO' EAVES·SHEWING GABLET·SILLS
SECTION·THRO' ARCH RINGS
CORBELLING·ON LEFT·SIDE·OF WEST·STACK·IN COURTYARD
BASE·OF CHIMNEY SHAFTS
CORBEL·AND·SPRING-ING·OF·ARCH·ON·RIGHT OF·GREAT·STACK
SET·BACK·ON LEFT·OF·GREAT STACK
QUARTER FULL·SIZE BRICK·DETAILS

FIREPLACE IN LONG GALLERY – EAST WING.

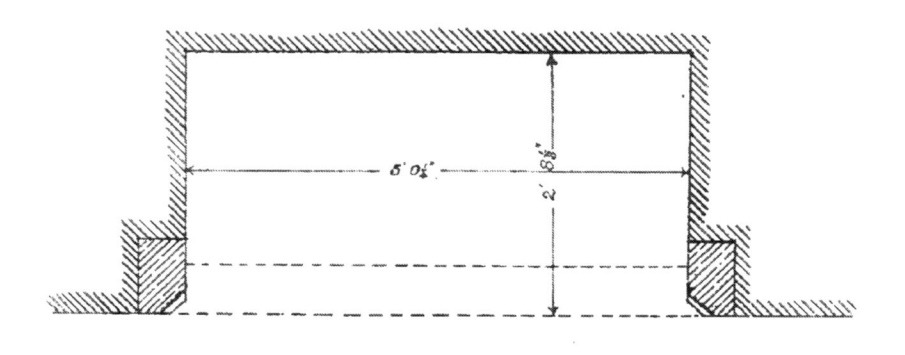

PLATE 14

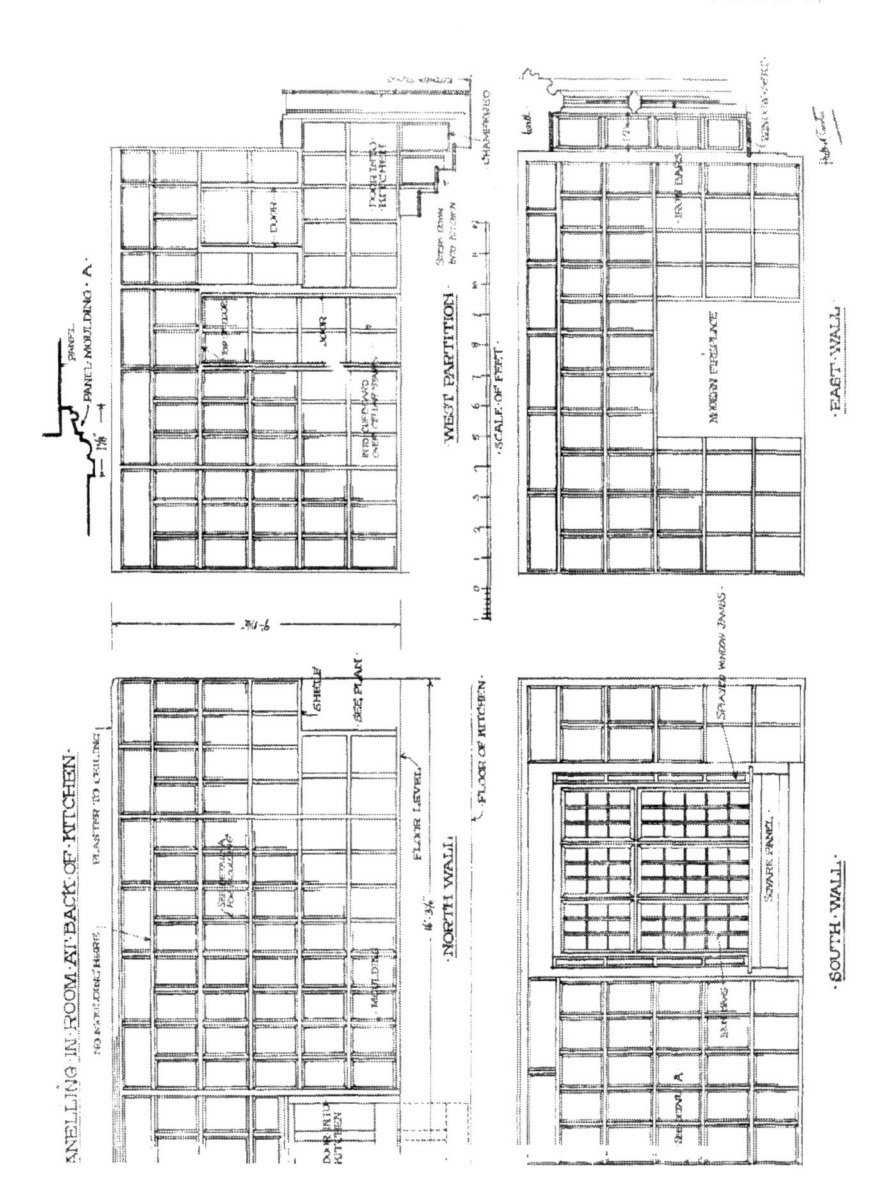

PLATE 15

SOUTH FRONT

PLATE 16

VIEW FROM SOUTH-WEST

PLATE 17

VIEW FROM SOUTH-EAST

PLATE 18

WEST FRONT AND SOUTH-WEST GABLE

PLATE 19

EAST AND NORTH FRONTS

ENTRANCE PORCH

PLATE 21

(a) ARCH UNDER CHIMNEY-STACK

(b) CORBELLING TO KITCHEN CHIMNEY-STACK

PLATE 22

STAIR-TURRET, ETC.

PLATE 23

ENTRANCE TO STAIRCASE TURRET

PLATE 24

ROOFS AND CHIMNEY SHAFTS

PLATE 25

(a) WINDOWS IN GABLE

(b) GARDEN ENTRANCE

PLATE 26

PANELLED ROOM, GROUND FLOOR

PLATE 27

(a) FIREPLACE, LONG GALLERY, FIRST FLOOR

(b) DETAIL OF SAME

PLATE 28

(a) SECOND FLOOR (OVER HALL)

(b) SECOND FLOOR (WEST WING)

(c) SECOND FLOOR, STAIRCASE

PLATE 29

BARN, INTERIOR

PLATE 30

PAINTED ROOM OVER HALL.
DRAWN BY T. H. CLARKE.

PLATE 31

PAINTED ROOM OVER HALL
(PHOTOGRAPH LENT BY THE ROYAL COMMISSION
ON HISTORICAL MONUMENTS—ENGLAND)

PLATE 32

PAINTINGS IN EAST WING (Second Floor)
DRAWN BY T. H. CLARKE

Lightning Source UK Ltd.
Milton Keynes UK
UKHW020805250521
384341UK00006B/490